Beyond the Castle

The Enchanted Forest

Beyond the Castle
The Enchanted Forest

By
Mavis Tofte

CREATIVE QUILL
Salem • Oregon

Copyright © 2002 by Mavis Tofte

All rights reserved. No part of this book may be used or reproduced in any manner whatsoever without the written permission of the author. Printed in the United States of America. For information contact: Creative Quill, 460 Myers St. Salem, Oregon 97302.

Library of Congress Control Number: 2002090984

ISBN: 0-9709906-1-8

First Edition 2002

Cascade Printing Company • Salem, Oregon

In memory of My Dad, Chester Bjorke, who passed away at the age of ninety two. The Enchanted Forest was his favorite place to visit as long as his health permitted. He would sit for hours talking to other guests at the picnic tables.

Contents

Foreword

Chapter One	Discovering the Lower Trail	11
Chapter Two	Tofteville	33
Chapter Three	The Haunted House	51
Chapter Four	Fairweather Theater	73
Chapter Five	Big Timber Log Ride	85
Chapter Six	Ice Mountain	97
Chapter Seven	The Old World Village	105
Chapter Eight	The Moods of Fantasy Fountains	115
Chapter Nine	Mother Nature	129
Chapter Ten	Rides For the Young & More	155
Chapter Eleven	Looking Back	163
Chapter Twelve	New Visions	175

Also by Mavis Tofte

The Enchanted Forest and Its Family
(A history, including photos)

FOREWORD

Many travelers have come to Oregon for its hunting and fishing. It was known as a sportsman's paradise. Over thirty years ago, when I was a young man, I had another type of dream for travelers to the state of Oregon. When I took my family to visit relatives in other states, we stopped at small roadside parks to take a break from driving. At that time, our State had little to offer the traveling family. My dreams of a different future took shape and grew. It seemed that Oregon had a need for another form of family entertainment that would appeal to local residents as well as travelers to our State.

Judging by what other states had to offer, Oregon had room to improve on its choices for family entertainment. I wanted to do something that would be more creative than my uninspiring drafting job for the highway department. My artistic talents desperately needed another more challenging outlet. With this in mind, the door was open for the creation of the Enchanted Forest theme park as a different source of fun for all ages. When the park first opened in 1971, due to limited funds, it started from humble beginnings. However, with passage of time, the Enchanted Forest became one of Oregon's leading tourist attractions.

It did not happen over night but only after years of hard work and perseverance. My whole family became involved in its operation and development. As the park's name suggests, it was built in the midst of nature's lush vegetation and all efforts have been made to preserve the forest. My hopes were that my efforts would bring another source for family activity that might add to the pleasure of others. The smiling faces and exciting chatter of visitors to the Enchanted Forest have been my reward. It was and still is so uplifting to see young and old enjoying the park facilities. There's a saying that expresses my feelings, "It makes my day!"

Roger Tofte

[Action] is the last resource of those who know how to dream
Oscar Wilde (1854-1900)

Chapter One
Discovering the Lower Trail

For those who grow weary of the massive, conglomerate theme parks located across the United States, there's a special treat for travelers visiting Oregon. The Enchanted Forest, Oregon's oldest family owned theme park, is located about seven miles south of Salem; the State Capitol. Many visitors to the state may not be aware of this little gem nestled in the hills south of Salem. This hillside treasure was not created by huge corporations or supported by government funds. It was built through the hard work and perseverance of a young family trying to make ends meet. This project was spearheaded by the Enchanted Forest's founder, Roger Tofte. He had the vision and artistic talents to create his dream for others to visit and enjoy. He discovered that it is possible to create something unique blending with nature's beauty without the support of multi-million dollar corporations. As Roger's wife, I ran the business during the early years and filled in where there was the most need.

Having said this, I would like to be your guide on a journey of discovery that starts with the lower trail. Our adventure begins at the Castle as our path winds its way through the forest leading to Tofteville (an old western town). The creations of man and the beauty of nature join in making this a unique experience for both young and old. Through the eye of the camera, I hope to help you explore some of the treasures that lie within this mystical land of enchantment. The lower trail is themed as a walk through the forest's land of fairy tales and storybook characters. Travelers will soon find there is more than what one sees at first glance. Hidden treasures abound for those who look beyond the scattered scenes along the trail.

Visitors who came to the forest park in 1971 when it first opened to the public will notice many changes have taken place on return visits. Some changes are to improve conditions, not just build new attractions. For example: one of those changes was the improvement of the path that our guests walked on. In the beginning, the pathway starting at the Castle was spread with cedar shavings that gave a fresh, woodsy smell to the trail. However, there were some drawbacks. For starters, it was hard to push strollers along the trail as one mushed their way up the hillside. But this was not the only problem. When it rained (after all this was Oregon), the wet cedar stuck to visitors shoes and was tracked into buildings making a yucky mess. To improve conditions for everyone, the trails have been resurfaced with paver stones or cement wherever possible which is better suited to Oregon's climate. It's not the "yellow brick road" of Oz but it is the way to travel through the Enchanted Forest.

As stated before, Oregon's Enchanted Forest is a family owned park. The family not only owns this forest park but also operates it. Our children and our grandchildren learned their basic work ethics at this forest park. There is ample opportunity to use their many talents while they grow and decide what they want to become in life. As the park grew so did our need for other workers and we were soon flooded with applications. It became a great learning experience for all, especially developing social skills in dealing with people. All employees learn to try to make each guest's visit an enjoyable one.

The creations of man and the beauty of nature join in making this journey a unique experience of these realities. Both young and old, children and adults, begin their trek through the forest at the Castle as they pass over the bridge that's built across the moat. If the visitor pauses long enough on the bridge to glance at the water below, a lazy alligator can be seen basking in the sun. Some visitors stop, make a wish and toss a few coins into the moat. Some guests don't stop for long, especially when eager children often dash ahead of their much slower parents.

Alligator in Castle moat

14 Beyond the Castle

Inside the Castle, a knight stands guard in his suit of armor. His sole duty is to see that the residents of the forest obey the rules of the Castle. He has plenty of time on his hands and knows all the gossip that lurks in the halls of his castle. He knows all about the Queen in her parlor eating bread and honey while the King is counting out his money. As for the Queen there may be a reason why she doesn't fit into her old clothes. With our knight, mums the word. So don't ask him any questions. His facial expression is hidden behind his armored mask. One wonders what he has on his mind. He's just not very talkative. This knight is harder to pry information from than the guards at Buckingham Palace. Of course his visor is down and who knows what he's actually thinking when he views the visitors passing in front of him. They cannot see his facial expressions. Think about it, you may be looking at this noble knight but he is also looking at you. Don't worry though, as stated before he keeps things to himself.

There is a quote about the matter of silence that the knight may have thoughts about.

It is a good practice to leave a few things unsaid.
           Elbert Hubbard (1856-1915): The Roycroft Dictionary and Book of Epigrams (1923)

Armored guard

Although the Castle is not large there are some interesting sights of the era for guests to view. Fairy tale scenes are shown in the narrow confines of the Castle halls.

16 Beyond the Castle

Old King Cole

The local news is posted on a bulletin board near the armored knight to keep folks up to date. Jack Be Nimble really has to watch out for those burning candlesticks! In those days they didn't have proper medical care that we enjoy today. The magic world of fairy tales unfolds before our eyes as we proceed on our journey. While exiting the Castle, a cheerful elf and bear cub show us the way. As we continue along the path, we truly discover this is only the beginning. The theme has been established as we explore what lays ahead.

A delightful world of fantasy greets visitors as some guests pause long enough to take pictures for their memories.

Discovering the Lower Trail 17

This Way

Soon we reach the Gingerbread House which brings back memories of the classic fairy tale, "Hansel and Gretel". The little house appears to be a delicious cake or giant ice-cream cone. It looks good enough to eat but I wouldn't recommend it for lunch. As Hansel and Gretel learned, looks can be deceiving. Inside, guests see the witch beckoning Gretel to help her. However, her trickery does not fool our young heroine. Other visitors stand close to the window trying to hear what is being said as the old hag does her best to deceive Hansel's sister. From what I hear Gretel has a few tricks up her sleeve, too. Many of you know how the story goes.

Maybe I can take a picture in here. It's dark within the house and the protective glass adds to the difficulty of getting a good photo with my ever ready camera. I couldn't capture the witch, but managed to take a photo of Gretel as she listens to the old crone.

Gretel inside the Gingerbread House

After we leave the little house, we soon reach the Rabbit Hole, the more cautious visitors hesitate. It looks very dark and who knows what happens to you when you go in there! The braver youngsters enter, sometimes dragging an adult along like a security blanket. Many a parent has accompanied their children through the ominous passage which exits through a key hole at the other end. Once they have accomplished this feat, the meek and shy are so excited that they frequently ask if they can do it again.

Such was the case some years ago when I remember seeing one youngster who was extremely afraid of going into the forbidding tunnel. After a lot of coaxing, he finally gathered

Discovering the Lower Trail 19

enough courage and decided to give it a very timid try. When he successfully came out the other end, this little one was so excited that he went through again and again. He didn't want to stop until his parents found out that they still had a lot more to see. There was and still is much more ahead for all ages, not just the fairy tales as each visitor soon discovers. These parents urged their son to leave the Rabbit Hole for it was time to move on. Their journey had just begun.

Rabbit Hole

In earlier years at the Enchanted Forest, our younger children often volunteered to guide those who were afraid of the dark passage. The darkness of this attraction often serves as a barometer to help decide later about going through the Haunted House. Both are dark, although they are two different experiences. At least the Rabbit Hole is underground and a frightened child cannot leap high into the air to clutch their parent around the neck. This has happened in the Haunted house.

Keyhole exit from Rabbit Hole

Discovering the Lower Trail 21

Guests to our park have noticed the attention given to details in each scene. The care given to creating quality in each endeavor was a labor of love on the part of its developer.

There's no doubt, this is a make-believe world. A watchful eye will catch some unusual sights that even Mother Nature didn't put there. For example, I see a gigantic butterfly on the side of a tree and there are flowers near the wonderland characters shaped like smiling pigs. The colorful surroundings and wide use of artistic imagination add to the total picture as we stroll along the trail.

Huge butterfly resting on tree trunk

Some visitors may not notice the butterfly because its resting place is rather dark. It depends on how much of the sun is on this tree. Guests often don't notice some things until their second or third time around. I couldn't resist snapping a picture of the nearby flowers. They seemed to brighten the day.

Smiling flowers

Unusual sights are the norm if one looks for them. I like the large yellow flowers that seem to be spreading their warmth on those walking by. Look! There's Alice as she looks up at the mushroom in her wonderland.

Mad Hatter's tea party

Among the residents of the lower trail are characters from Alice in Wonderland, Jack and Jill, Snow White, and others. Before long, the Dwarf's Cottage appears ahead of us as we come around a bend in the trail. This is a very popular spot for the little ones who can look in the windows that are at their level. As for the rest of us, if one stoops to look in the window, there is

Snow White singing and sweeping the floor as she tries to tidy up for her seven messy friends.

She's in a cozy family room where one of her forest friends is playing the organ. Snow White is alone for the moment while her seven benefactors are working in the mine. The picture of her is taken through glass. Just around the corner, visitors can get a peek into the Dwarf's bedroom on the second floor. The cottage is a favorite of the young and the young at heart.

Snow White

Discovering the Lower Trail 25

Waterfall in mine

Further along the trail is the Dwarf's mine and the walk-through Witches Head. The black lights in the mine cast interesting colors on one's clothing such as white shoe laces. Youngsters love to look at their ink stamped hands which glow in the darkness of the mine. Colorful waterfalls shed enough light to help guests find their way through the dark passages. Dwarf's are seen working as one leaves this area. However, the shadows inside the mine tend to give them an eerie appearance.

26 Beyond the Castle

Spooky dwarfs working in mine

After leaving the mine I happen to hear a lot of commotion in the leafy greenery above me. It is still early in the morning and the sun is filtering through the tangle of honeycomb branches and overhead foliage. It is a beautiful day for a walk! Though this is the land of fairy tales, Mother Nature has a hand in its design.

As we continue on we are greeted by squeals of laughter from children sliding out of the Witches Head and we pause long enough to enjoy the expressions on their faces. Visitors can walk into the head of this structure and proceed to the upper level where they can either slide out or walk down a walkway to the side.

The creative Witches Head became one of the original trademarks of the Enchanted Forest.

Witches Head

Nearby, an ancient log fell across the trail forming a natural overpass for our guests to walk under as they continue toward the Three Bears House. Small trees are sprouting upward from the fallen log.

Log overpass

Those who rush on may not notice the subtle charm of surrounding vegetation. Low moss covered branches hide other forest treasures from our sight. The birds in all their glory are chirping far above and can be heard but not seen. I look and search the area directly over my head but to no avail. My attention is drawn to the shrill sound of birds gleefully communicating to each other in their own world in the overhead foliage. They are well hidden from my probing eyes. The dense growth not only shelters the birds, it also adds to the quiet charm of this mystical land.

At different times of the year, a variety of flowers can be seen in the forest. I've seen Rhododendrons, wild strawberry plants, Mountain Ash, wild Columbine, Dogwood, and many more. Each adds a bonus to ones trek along the trail. Further along the path, near the Three Bears House and other wooded scenes, nature adds to the serenity and peace one feels while visiting the Enchanted Forest. If the visitor pauses long enough, he or she may get a glimpse of a salamander or small fish in the pond near the bear's house. Lately, a young deer has been spotted resting on the bank by the water's edge. I might even get a picture of it with my camera. There it is, just below us among the ferns. You never know what mysteries might be uncovered in this truly enchanted forest.

Deer hidden near pond

30   Beyond the Castle

Three Bears House

Guests who came to visit our park in the early years may remember an interesting structure built across the trail near the Three Bears house. It was designed similar to a wishing well. However, Father Time stepped in and the quaint well look-alike deteriorated with the passage of time and exposure to the elements. It died of old age and was never replaced. Its wooden structure reached the point that it was necessary to remove it. Visitors threw coins into the nearby pond to make their wishes. Guests still do this today as well as making their wishes at the Castle moat. This is only a sample of how the Enchanted Forest is constantly undergoing change.

Crooked House

We soon come upon the forest's Crooked House and its challenge to the visitor's sense of balance. I watch as a toddler struggles through wobbling from side to side. Others watching couldn't control their laughter. We often learn from children to enjoy the simple things in life.

As we continue along the trail, we come upon the Shoe Slide. This is one of several slides in the park and guests can ride their magic carpets to the bottom. You'll usually see relatives taking pictures as friends enjoy this pastime. What a popular attraction for both children and adults. There's an expression "act your age". In this forest park the gap narrows between the young and the old. Perhaps a better adage would be you're as young as you feel. In this world, all become young as they relive memories of days gone by.

Shoe Slide

We have just finished what is commonly referred to as the lower trail. Beyond this point, the visitor will move into a different area of the park. It will be the Enchanted Forest's western town called Tofteville. A sign behind the Shoe Slide tells us which way to go.

The following quote applies to the Enchanted Forest theme park.

If a man write a better book, preach a better sermon, or make a better mouse-trap than his neighbor, tho' he build his house in the woods, the world will make a beaten path to his door.
Ralph Waldo Emerson 1803-82

Chapter Two
Tofteville

As visitors move beyond the Shoe Slide, they are greeted by a sign that reads "Tofteville". At this point the trail leads us to another section of the Enchanted Forest. It gives us a glimpse into a different period of time that depicts the old west. Though the town is not large, it displays some of the things that might have existed in the days of yesteryear on the frontier.

Welcome sign

We continue our journey of exploration by searching for reminders of this era in our past. Let's start our rounds by walking up the steps to follow the board walk around the perimeter of

Tofteville. There are tongue-in-cheek glimpses into life as it might have been in those days while visitors look through windows along the walkway. One of the sights could be of the laundry which may have seen rather strange use in its time.

Ma Cruddy's laundry

Another sight is the sheriff's office. Perhaps the sheriff might make an appearance even though he is trying to mount a campaign for re-election. He said his run for office is based on his record.

Tofteville   35

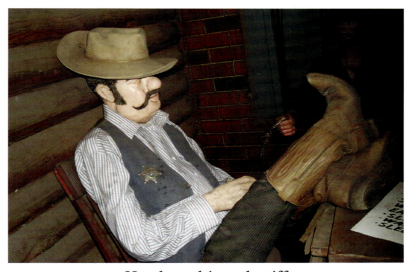

Hard working sheriff

Few people realize what a difficult task it is to run for office in a tough town like Tofteville. Local residents don't seem to understand the many duties that are required to keep the peace. The sheriff is mounting a serious bid for re-election. However, there seems to be some doubt about who might run against him. What a thankless job he has of serving the community and tending to his own affairs at the same time. The stress of the work does take its toll. Perhaps his constituents would better understand his situation if he had the local sign company make up a poster to state more clearly his intentions and his best qualities. Use your own judgment when considering his skills and abilities.

Guests may be able to read one of the posters which declares the sheriff's honorable intentions and lists a few of his notable qualifications. Hm-m-m, well, what can you expect considering the times and the quality of other candidates who come from the same mold.

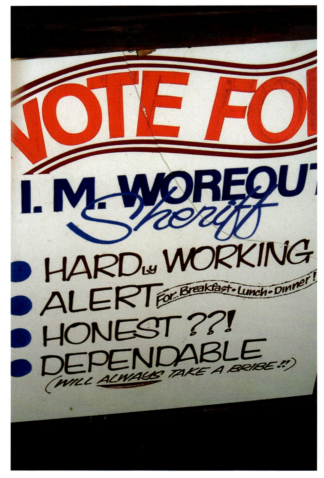

Sheriff's campaign poster

It is rumored that the local undertaker might consider running for office. However, some citizens think he may have a conflict of interest.

They say he's a little trigger happy and may only dispel justice in a way favorable to his already thriving business.

Not far from the sheriff's office, guests get a quick look at the dangers that lurk in the shadows for any business in the wild west. While walking past the Fells Wargo office, one might notice that the agent is having problems. Of course I'm guessing, but I don't think he can count on the sheriff to come to his rescue.

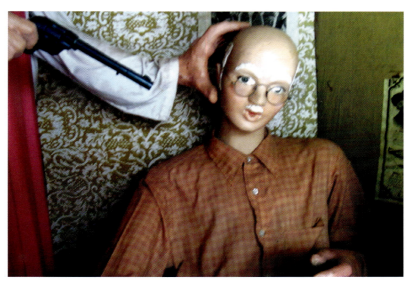

Intruder at Fells Wargo office

Life then was definitely not as we know it today. There weren't inspectors to regulate business activity. There was no TV, no movies, no advanced medical care, or many of the conveniences that we now take for granted. The laundry, the boarding house, the barber, the dentist, the funeral parlor had their own rules and they determined how they would conduct their own business affairs in Tofteville. Gun shot justice seemed to be the rule of the day. It was a way of life on the frontier which can be verified by taking a look at the rugged boot hill located on the edge of town.

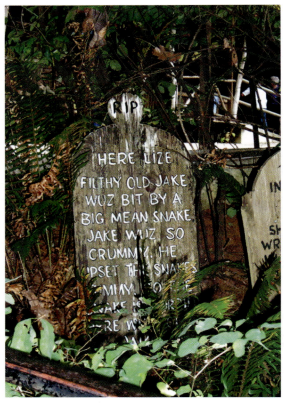

Boot Hill marker

Further down the street, there's more to see. Let's take a stroll into the General Store to check out the merchandise. There's plenty to attract the eager shopper.

General Store

Since there's a lot of ground to cover, let's shop later. It might be easier to carry our packages then. What's next? A bit further down the board walk is the dentist's office. From what I've heard, he's rather absent-minded and somewhat shaky. I wouldn't recommend his services to the newcomers in town.

Dentist, the only choice

Across the street is the barber's shop where a young novice practices his skills on the latest hair styles from east of the Mississippi. He recently moved here from Dodge City where his skills were not appreciated. The young man did too much day dreaming while on the job. From the local gossip, I heard that prospectors and others didn't like the best hair styles from the east. Beaver hats and slicked down hair were not on their list for a good looking frontiersman.

There might be some in town who would accept his new fangled styles but you know how people talk. Perhaps they wouldn't be as irritable as his former customers. A word of advice, the barber should keep his mind on his work. Trembling hands are not welcome in this trade. How long will he last? Hm-m, we'll see.

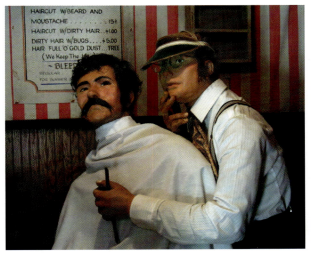

Hesitant barber

The next exhibit might be overlooked, but claims to be of interest to those who have a strange fascination for history that is bent a little. The unique Tofteville Muzium is not like any other. Some relics might be recognized but there are others that give food for thought to perplexed souls. There are a few displays that might seem a little wacko. So, what can you expect in the old west?

Inside there used to be a Native American beaded shirt hanging on the wall. Although quite ornate, it was not authentic. This shirt was made and decorated by our son for a Cub Scout project. However, all his hard work attracted the wrong kind of attention. The garment was stolen early in the parks existence. Since it was one of a kind, it was never replaced.

For those who might not recognize the place, I took a shot with my camera on the possibility that the traveler might want to check out the inside.

Tofteville Muzium

Let's take a quick look inside and see what the Muzium holds today. Well, there are some

Tofteville 43

interesting items in this small collector's room. For example, the weathered military saddle has seen better days. Looks like the well known sculptor, A. Beaver, has another classic on display. They say he may have a private showing soon. One never knows how or when talent will show itself.

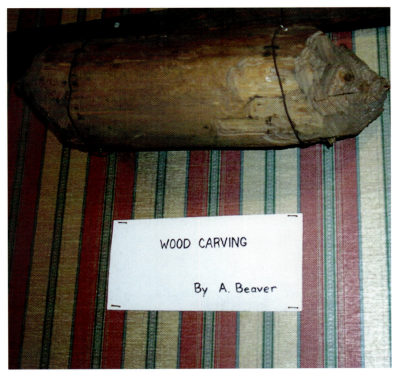

Carving by A. Beaver

44   Beyond the Castle

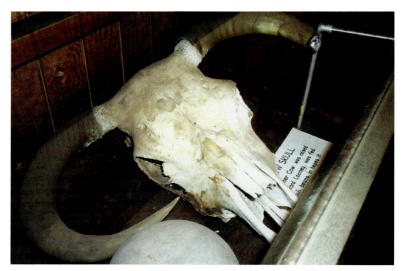

Found in the desert

The Muzium showcase includes an old cattle skull collected from the desert. Cattle thieves better know as "Rustlers" no longer have an interest in this critter. This relic of days gone by is a little too old for their tastes. Fortunately, this old fellow found a home at the Enchanted Forest.

I see something called a cherry pitter and there's a long saw used by the old timers when they were logging. Usually, an old photo can be spotted among the smaller items in the room. As I look about, it makes me wonder why people in old pictures seldom smile. But like I said this is a small Muzium and it won't take long to read about the relics on display. Let's move on to the Opera House. It's just a few doors down.

Wagon Wheel Opera House

In the center of Tofteville is the Wagon Wheel Opera House where shoppers can pick up souvenirs. It is also a gathering place with benches outside for those who are waiting for others. Through the years, the Opera House has undergone many changes as its needs changed. The old stage outgrew its usefulness and was removed. As with business today, growth usually means some kind of change. It's the same for Tofteville.

Let's take a peek inside. There might be something you would like to purchase. I think there's a book in the store called *The Enchanted Forest and Its Family* which gives a history of the park from its beginning. I've heard it makes a great gift.

46   Beyond the Castle

Player piano with a history

If the player piano is rolling out its tunes, the place can be jumping with music of the west such as "Buffalo Gals". The continuous playing of these dated tunes and repetitious sounds can loose their appeal to employees working in the Opera House. Rumors say that dance hall girls used to do their dancing on top of the piano causing the scratches found there. This conjures up memories of old dance halls and boisterous saloons. Many a cowpoke has staggered through the old halls much as one might walk through Tofteville's one and only, Mc Goon's saloon. High class entertainment is not a priority in this replica of a western town. Whether fact or fiction, one accepts what they feel has the most appeal to them. Dance Hall girls no longer work in Tofteville. The story is only fabricated history.

Shooting Gallery

There are activities in Tofteville to test ones skills such as the Shooting Gallery, Quick Draw, and the target boat steering controls. Quick Draw speaks his own lingo to challenge visitors who pass near his domain. He might refer to an unsuspecting victim as a "wall-eyed lizard" and make similar comments about his shooting abilities. Usually a crowd gathers to take him up on his bragging taunts. Many a city slicker has faced the boasting gunslinger.
    My only chance to get a picture of the Shooting Gallery is to take it before the park opens to visitors. Pictures can not be taken when its open because flashes from cameras can play havoc with electrical devices.

Cave entrance

Fort Fearless is at one end of town and just beyond is the Indian Caves with its underground tunnel. One of the exits comes out through the fire logs in the tepee. It's a great place for the Tom Sawyer in every child. There is more than one way to leave the caves which can be confusing to parents who are tired of waiting for their youngster to emerge. If they get too impatient and enter at one place, their child most likely will come out from another. This is a real attraction for those with an exploring nature.

On the outside, there are holes in the upper wall that give the appearance of a skull. Sometimes this is harder to distinguish because of the mossy overgrowth.

Indian Caves' mystery skull

50   Beyond the Castle

Let's wander back through Tofteville and go beyond the massive livery stable doors at the other end. It's not far and what we visit next will be different than anything we have seen so far. This will take us to a more ominous attraction at the Enchanted Forest. On the way we might take a look at Bryan's Plaque.

Bryan's Plaque

This plaque was placed at the Enchanted Forest as a memorial to Bryan's short life. He always wanted to come here for a vacation. Unfortunately, he had a fatal accident on his first day of school. This little fellow was only six at the time of his passing. It is located between the Haunted House and Tofteville.

Chapter Three
The Haunted House

    Nestled among the trees on the other side of Tofteville is a brick walkway that leads us to a weathered old house. The surrounding trees tend to hide most of it. Its ominous presence seems to emanate a message of foreboding. The cracked window panes and battered, sagging shutters hint at something mysterious within its aging walls. Neglected moss covered rails guide the visitor to the steps leading to the Haunted House of the Enchanted Forest and all that exists within. At this point, the faint of heart may have second thoughts about entering to explore such an uninviting building.

Walkway to Haunted House

It's a house with a history of deception and illusion that is used as a form of entertainment.

Haunted House shattered window

The Haunted House

Haunted House, a different view

One look at the outside and we are aware that this structure is definitely not a candidate for "House Beautiful". If such a magazine exists, this Enchanted Forest house might be qualified for something called "House Ugly". It should be noted that in 1991, "Inside Track's" fifth annual readers' poll listed this Haunted House as the best "walk-thru". Its dark and somber setting invites the inquisitive to explore this mansion of intrigue and mystery. With the aid of the camera's eye, I have tried to capture the mood of the Haunted House. Some people have a fear of dark and eerie places and from these photos they will be able to get an idea of what they are missing. For others, it will recall memories of past visits. The unknown within will only be partially portrayed. Interior black light effects can not effectively be caught by the ever watchful eye of my camera. Let's proceed up the steps. I'll be your guide.

Entrance to the Haunted House

At this point, we push aside the dark, protective curtain to the entry hallway and are greeted by the deep sounds of an organ playing, issuing from the music room to the right. It could be the sound of a church organ but this is no church. After a second look, one notices that the hands moving over the keys don't seem to be attached to anyone. Is this a clue to what lays ahead? We cautiously glance down the hall to assess what might be next. There in glowing lights an eerie figure appears to be beckoning us to venture further into the unknown.

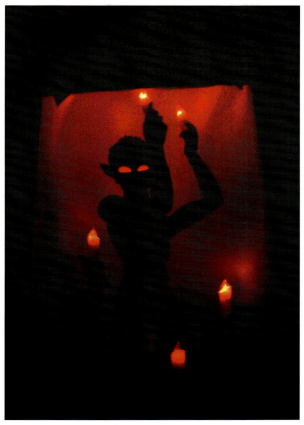

Beckoning spirit

56 Beyond the Castle

Fear not, we have just begun our journey. There are plenty of somber pictures on the wall of former residents. Eyes seem to follow us wherever we go. Wait! Is that an empty picture frame? No, on closer examination, one sees that there is something there. Or is it? Are our senses to be trusted? Dark shadows leave much to the imagination and judgment tends to stray from reality. Oops, another visitor just bumped into me. Well, it's time to move on to the living room that lies dead ahead. The décor and furnishings are definitely not from "House Beautiful". The presence within these walls is threatening the senses. Decorative chandeliers hang over our heads that add just enough light to almost see other guests nearby. The legs tremble, the heart beats faster, and eyes open wider trying to penetrate the darkness of the dimly lit room. There are several figures in the room that are not park visitors. One prominent figure looms above the others. His cape makes him seem to be someone of authority. His stern face and staring eyes do not seem to welcome us. He appears to be a protective guardian of the living room which causes us to proceed with caution. It's rumored that this distinguished gentleman was a former Professor of Anthropology at Salem's Willamette University. At least that's what I heard. Who knows what truth lies behind such rumors.

Living room guardian

Next to him sits a figure that seems old and frail. Oh! No! It suddenly moves and rises to a towering height. Other guests in the room jump or scream in startled response.

Stairs leaving living room

One exits this area by taking the red, carpeted stairs to the right. People move cautiously. Some are not too sure whether they should advance or retreat. A sound of thunder pierces the air ahead of us. There's another watchful picture on the wall. Was it of a former butler? Your guess is as good as mine.

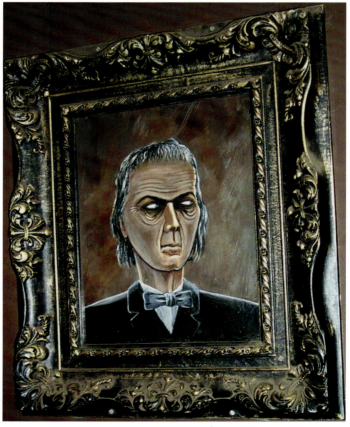

The butler

Graveyard for those who stayed permanently

    A glassed in area to the left allows the explorer who lingers to view the Haunted House graveyard that may be the last resting place of former employees or visitors who never, ever left this house with its chilling charm. A bolt of lightning enhances the drifting specters issuing forth from crooked tombstones. A shudder briefly grips the soul as another dark shadow appears on the wall. However, no one is there. The imagination is a powerful tool. Shadows and eyes that follow your movement through the hall could be just around the corner. When workers close the Haunted House at night, they often feel there is someone else inside when no one is supposed to be there. They make their closing rounds quickly.

The Haunted House 61

A lingering shadow

Other discoveries are made as one turns the corner. An object appears in a hole in the wall. Is it a head? No! But it was! Visitors are greeted by a skull's toothy grin, no doubt, recalling the glory of a past life. The thatch of dark hair gives no clue that this was once Lillian, an 1872 beauty queen. The shadows of her past life are no longer reflected in the vacant stare of this Haunted House resident. There seems to be a chill in the air as a slight shudder finds its target.

So, here's to Lillian, Queen of the Haunted House hallways.

Lillian, 1872 Beauty Queen

I feel something softly touch my hand and discover a child standing there. He grabs my arm and only wants to continue if I go with him. Of course, I'll take him. Sure! There's nothing to fear. Our tour of deception continues. Who were those people from another life or another time in history? Shades of Boris Karlof, was there any connection? What happened to all those other visitors or long forgotten employees? We'll probably never really know.

Hall monitor

As we climb the stairs, we notice a hall mirror over a small landing that reflects swaying candelabra. I look around and again there aren't any candelabra to be seen beyond the mirror. That's strange.

Mysterious mirror

Oh! No! I think that's a picture of somebody's relative. She doesn't seem very friendly.

Look out for Aunt Matilda

The child at my side is anxious and we move a little quicker. He is startled when we turn the corner and see a scene showing a headless man well, not exactly. The strange chessboard in front of him suggests another kind of game or player. As we listen to the man saying something about being beside himself, a loud sound from above startles us as an axe swings in a threatening manner over our heads. The child's grip grows tighter than before.

Headless Man

A bedroom scene is a little more soothing to the nerves even though things are not what they seem. However, my hand is still in a tight grasp as we move up a few steps taking us even higher in the attic. We hear a shrill sound as something white flashes toward us. My young partner nearly jumps out of his shoes. Then he starts to pull back, but on second thought, the young man decides that it is better to move on than to retreat.

Attic ghoul

Another poor soul appears in a hole in the wall to mark our passing. We move swiftly pass other residents and barely pause at the man eating plant room, better know as the house solarium.

Hungry plants

Quickly descending some steps, we come upon the Haunted House kitchen. One look tells us that it would have trouble passing inspection from the health department as a food service area. It couldn't possibly rate an A, B, or even a conditional C. However, it might qualify for a special D rating for "doomed".

Doomed kitchen

By this time, the child with me is getting anxious to leave the Haunted House and enter the real world again. On the way out, there are plenty of other sights and sounds to soothe our senses in a fractured way. We come upon a couple of skeleton prisoners, who used to be drinking buddies, singing a departing rendition as we near the exit tunnel. These skeletons are retired entertainers and still enjoy performing. My junior partner is not interested in these two former gentlemen and urges me to quicken my pace. I smiled as we headed toward the next passage. The exit tunnel is just around the corner. I assure him it won't be long now. We bid adieu to the two skeletons who were still trying to entertain others walking by their dungeon. I did manage to get their photo for memories sake which I am only too glad to show you.

This is the photo that I was able to get of the skeletons before entering the tunnel.

Singing buddies

We carefully pass by what must have been a glimpse of the former "employee's lounge" with someone in there taking a break.

The Haunted House 71

Employee's lounge

The residents of the Haunted House are many. What restless bidding has caused their return to this place in their present form? What judgment has placed them here to serve their time on earth?

Finally, we pass through the squeaking exit gate and feel the warm sunlight on our skin.

There is the Tofteville livery stable across the street where we first passed through to start our trek to the Haunted House. As the saying goes, what goes around comes around. This is the real world with living, breathing people walking about. The boy releases his tight grip and races to waiting relatives. He breathlessly tries to explain the sights and sounds of what he has just experienced. As for me, it's time to turn the camera off and take a well earned break.

Livery stable gate leading to the Haunted House

Chapter Four
Fairweather Theater

If you are ready for a change of pace, the Enchanted Forest offers another form of entertainment. It consists of live performances of fairy tale spoofs at the outdoor theater.

Fairweather Theater

The stage is found on a hillside among the trees with wooden benches for the audience. The seats follow the natural slope of the hill giving the spectators a good view of the stage below. The surrounding majestic trees form a perfect setting for the performing arts. Here, one sees comedy in its purest form—live. Because the plays are live, nobody knows what may happen that is not in the script. With the guidance of their director,

Susan Vaslev, it is an excellent training ground for aspiring young actors. They also learn how to interact with the audience which is fun for both the actors and the spectators.

Susan Vaslev, Director, and Snow White

Fairweather Theater

Hopeful actors audition each year for a chance to perform during the upcoming season. The play for the 2001 season was "Snow White and the Seven Dorks". There are about four performances a day, weather permitting. The fresh air comedy strikes a balance between the interests of young children and the more subtle humor of the adults.

Trees at theater before audience arrives

76   Beyond the Castle

Since I've got my camera, let's take a look backstage. Snow White is there putting on her make up for the next performance. The Dorks are found just around the corner, I decided to take a photo of them backstage, waiting for their turn to go on.

Snow White getting ready

Fairweather Theater 77

The Seven Dorks backstage, waiting

What would the backstage be without its props, costumes, and necessary equipment? In these types of productions, wigs are almost a necessity. This is what the actors see. It may seem like clutter but there isn't always time to pick up. However, it is important to know where everything is. A lost prop could be a problem.

Wigs and props backstage

A thread and needle, a sewing machine, safety pins, or whatever it takes to mend costumes are all useful items. Make-up, costumes, parts of sets, an updated script might be needed-whatever it takes to put the show on could be found in the small area behind the stage area. On a hot day, there might be an occasional can of pop on the counter or someone's lunch. There's a time and place for everything, especially when the show is going on. Performers must be alert when listening for their entrance cue.

Backstage work area

As show time approaches, the audience gathers on the benches. Many stop at the nearby snack bar to grab a bite before the play starts. There's a lot of chattering going on while everyone waits for the music to begin which indicates it's almost showtime.

Vain Queen and magic mirror, 2001

Dancing Queen and huntsman

The show gets under way as the performers move into their roles. The actors interact with the audience much to the delight of the children. The children can't seem to get enough and by interaction they are drawn further into the story. Guests might even discover one of the performers sitting next to them as the actors depart from the stage setting. Due to aerobic stunts, Enchanted Forest actors need to know how to take a fall; also some of the scenes require an exhausting performance. This is in part why the number of daily shows is limited.

Actors in motion

Snow White and Seven Dorks, 2001

Fairweather Theater   83

In the previous scene, Snow White is a hit with the audience as she leaps through the air. On one of the earlier shows things got so crazy that one of the Dorks lost his head and it rolled toward the audience. The spectators roared! Performers often ask the children on the benches for their help and might even move out among them to the delight of the youngsters.

2001 cast saying goodbye to the audience

The weather was great for the 2001 season and most scheduled plays were presented. There is no admission charge for this added benefit to the park. However, currently there is one slight drawback to this attraction. Because the stage is built on a hillside, it is quite a walk up the slope. Though tiring, it is well worth the hike. On a hot day, visitors can get thirsty and hungry after arriving at the theater. In the early years, guests had to walk all the way back to Tofteville for drinks or a snack. Therefore, for the convenience of our visitors, a snack bar was added near the theater. Hunger pangs and thirst can now be satisfied without the long hike.

Theater Snack Bar

Even the snack bar's setting blends into the forest. At this point, it's about time to move on. Be sure to pick up your belongings before we leave the theater. It's a long way back. There is still more for us to see and do around the park.

Chapter Five
Big Timber Log Ride

Shrill screams fill the air as we approach the next attraction. A huge wooden structure looms in front of us called the Big Timber log ride. This log flume ride is outstanding for the thrills it gives the riders. It is currently the largest one of its kind in the northwest.

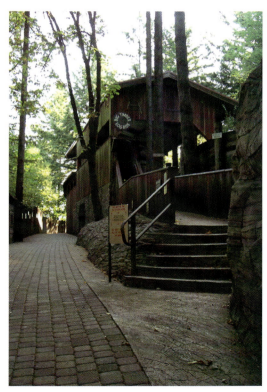

Entrance to Big Timber

Along the walkway to Big Timber is a high planked fence lined with nostalgic signs and posters of the past. Near the ride is a prospector tending to a "panning for treasure" trough where guests can try their luck for a prize. Although I'll not ride Big Timber, I'll use my camera to try to depict what this ride entails for those who are as cautious as me. When riders are loaded into their log, they are given a choice of whether or not they want to wear a protective poncho. This eases the possibility of getting wet during the descent into water at the end of the ride. The more adventurous want to tough it out. For them getting wet is part of the fun, especially on a hot summer day. Some are having so much fun that they go several times before moving on to other attractions. There is a size restriction and the very young cannot ride alone. As for me, I would probably have my eyes closed all the way and a grip so tight that one might call me a white knuckle rider.

For relatives and friends there is an observation deck located at the far end of the building where the logs splash down in to a receiving pond. Guests often take pictures from this advantage point. I've taken pictures of our own grandchildren from here. It is a lot of fun watching the different riders as they hit the water. Some try to show others that getting a little wet doesn't bother them. Others hide behind protective ponchos. Their expressions vary from extremely animated to stoic.

Big Timber Log Ride

Big Timber log ride

Those who wish to ride, climb the steps to the loading platform where they decide if they want to wear the protective gear before the attendant helps them settle into their log. When everyone is ready, the log is released and the guests are on their way up the mountain. With the aid of the camera, I am able to capture one of the logs ascending up the flume to wend its way through the upper woods and the mill.

Log ascending to the mill

With camera in tow, I hitch a ride with one of the workers who drives me up to the mill area. The logs and riders will pass through the mill on their journey around the logging area. I must crawl under the flume in order to get a better view and explore the possibilities for taking a few photos. I discover an animated logging camp with functioning equipment. By crawling around in the logging mill and trying to avoid water splashing over the side of the flume, I manage to take some pictures often ducking as the logs passed by over my head.

Switchman in action

Spinning blade

Across from the switchman is another platform with a working saw blade and other equipment. This is an actual saw from an old log mill that is activated for the riders to view as they pass by. There are also other pieces of equipment and tools reminiscent of days gone by. Another logger has his hands full as he works near the opening of the mill. One look tells us that he probably hasn't seen a razor in a long time. We could recommend the barbershop in Tofteville. But in this case, it's better to let sleeping dogs lay. Judging from the looks on these men's faces, I don't think they believe in the old adage to whistle while you work.

Big Timber Log Ride 91

Busy logger

Tools of the trade

Big Timber Log Ride   93

After passing through the mill, the log flume takes a sudden dip downward. The unexpected plunge prior to the main drop brings about some gasps and screams from the riders. I don't know how much sight seeing the guests are doing, but as long as I'm here I'll get an overview of the ride from above.

Upper view of log ride

There are also some wild flowers up here that are interesting. Look, I see some daisies under the flume. Guess I'll take their pictures too for memories sake. The next time one ventures up here, the flowers might not be around.

Daisies under log ride

As the rider enters the last plunge down the flume, there is an old dynamite shack to one side of the log ride. It is one of the last sights seen as our guests approach the end of the ride. They really aren't taking time to watch the scenery as they careen toward the receiving pond. The final splash raises high above their heads.

It's time to bid farewell to our current venture and investigate what lies ahead.

Big Timber Log Ride 95

Dynamite shack

One last thought before we move on. It seems to apply to many of us whether we're brilliant or not.

It may be those who do most, dream most.
—Stephen Leacock

Chapter Six
Ice Mountain

After leaving the rugged logging camp and its exciting Enchanted Forest log flume ride, we enter another section of the park. How do you feel about snow country and the mountains?

Ice Mountain

The majestic Ice Mountain is our next planned stop on our trek around the Enchanted Forest. In 1982 the popular Ice Mountain bobsled ride opened to the public where one can experience a Nordic event without leaving the Willamette Valley. This was the first major ride built at the park and was another change from what the park had up to that time. The white mountain peak has an alluring charm of its own not evident in any other area of the forest.

Near the mountain is a stylish alpine building that is the loading area for this thrilling ride through snow country. Two tracks are available to alleviate the length of time visitors spend waiting in line. Many guests are glad to see a few benches for those on the waiting deck below the ride. It's a good place to sit and rest after the long walk we've been enjoying. It's also a great place to watch the returning bobsleds. Friends and relatives are busy with their cameras. Onlookers may recognize their friends but can't hear them since they are enclosed in their bobsled by a clear hood for safety. While watching the bobsleds climb the mountain I can see a spray of mist released near the top of the track when the sled triggers a mechanism. The riders can catch sight of a cascading stream beside the track. This scenic stream is not visible to those who wait below. However, it adds to the mountain scenery as visitors begin their ride. Although some people may not be that intent upon the scenery as they zip around the mountain.

Ice Mountain 99

Mountain stream

When this popular attraction first opened the snow white peaks could be seen from the road as visitors drove to the Enchanted Forest. Now the park trees have grown so much that they conceal the alabaster peaks.

Alpine building

Pictured above is a glimpse of the alpine building where tickets are taken and passengers loaded into the waiting bob sleds. It is a small reminder of a different type of countryside more suggestive of snow country than the theme park where it is found. This picture was taken in the morning before the park opened for the day thus making better use of the light.

Ice Mountain 101

Ice Mountain in early morning

Many riders prefer to come early before the crowd collects later in the day. These visitors start at the mountain first before seeing the rest of the park. This is one way to take advantage of the smaller morning crowds. Later in the day, as others find out, this attraction becomes quite crowded and the lower waiting deck is jammed with onlookers. When I come back later the area will probably be so packed that it will be hard to take a picture without someone looming in front of the camera. That's the breaks.

102 Beyond the Castle

Early in the morning before guests arrive

Steam rising early in the day

Ice Mountain 103

I am waiting for someone to finish their ride and then we will gather ourselves in order to continue our rounds. Our group may have to stop soon for lunch. The upcoming village will be a refreshing change of pace from the rides.

One last look, Ice Mountain

You see things; and you say "Why?" But I dream things that never were; and I say "Why not?"
George Bernard Shaw 1856-1950

Chapter Seven
The Old World Village

They say variety is the spice of life and this is especially true when visiting the Enchanted Forest. After investigating the Big Timber log ride and Ice Mountain, visitors will experience a refreshing change of pace as they stroll through the Old World Village. Originally this section of the park was called the English Village but the name seemed to be too restrictive in scope. It is themed to take guests back to the renaissance period. Where would the literary world be without tales of Pinocchio, Robin Hood, and Camelot? The Brothers Grimm, Charles Dickens and Hans Anderson spin their tales of days gone by that add to the richness of our life today. Imagination and folk lore combine to give a foundation for the enhancement of our park. Let's take this journey back in time as we stroll through the streets of the Old World Village.

Looking about, we notice gossiping figures poking their heads out of the upper story windows to share the latest news. It's definitely more interesting to eavesdrop than wait for the town crier to make rounds later. As we walk down the cobble street, shops with nooks and crannies offer inviting places to explore. The winding street leads visitors through this world of yesteryear with its unique attention to quirky designs of chimneys, doorways, roofs, and overpasses. The steeples and spires each have their own appeal for those who notice the craft and detail in each structure. It's a pleasure to realize what patience and skill the builder, Roger Tofte, used in planning and creating this part of his dream world. It took true dedication and love of his work to achieve his goals. In this world of days gone by, one can get a glimpse of Geppetto, the Blackbird Bakery, Pinocchio's Playroom, Fantasy Fountains, and so forth.

Gossiping woman

On one side of the street is an enclosed contraption called the "Gravity Factory". Steel balls roll around a twisted track with their progress controlled by the trip action of odds and ends often found in the kitchen or shop. It's really fun to watch the tumbling orbs crash about in their unending journey to who knows where. This fascinating mechanism is similar to that of a Rube Goldberg invention with all its twists and turns. Guests who want to watch this activity must push a button to start the action.

Gravity Factory

Just around the corner is the entrance to Pinocchio's Play Room where park visitors walk up the steps to investigate the premises. The Three blind Mice are one of the first sights, but it is only the beginning. There are several hands on attractions in this area. Further up the stairs is a gigantic wooden keyboard that is playable. Of course visitors can get a few laughs when they get a view of themselves in the crooked mirrors on one side of a passage. There is a wall that has a rare collection of ancient puppets which seem to be dancing. They are antiques and an interesting feature for guests to enjoy. This is a collector's gift to the Enchanted Forest. We are thankful to those who have their own special way to show their appreciation of this magical park in their midst.

Special features like this only add to the enjoyment of park guests.

Rare puppet collection

Some visitors discover there is a very intriguing figure that might be overlooked because it is so small. This miniscule attraction is located in a very small square hole in the wall. If one looks in the hole, a dancing leprechaun can be seen. The invitation is there; try to catch him if you can. It's so simple. All one has to do is reach in and grab him, if it's possible. Guests soon discover that he's an illusive little fellow. It only proves the old saying that looks can be deceiving. However, it is a fun thing to try and it's one of many challenges located in the Enchanted Forest.
Look on it as a mini challenge found only in Pinocchio's Play Room.

Dancing leprechaun

Beyond this area, guests walk along a narrow passage to the miniature train room. One is greeted by a panoramic scene behind a glass partition. The glass is a little tricky and makes it difficult to take pictures but I will give it a try anyway. These photos may give you a better idea about what can be expected when you visit the train room. There are various buttons visitors push to activate items in the enclosed diorama. Visitors need only try them to see what happens.

110 Beyond the Castle

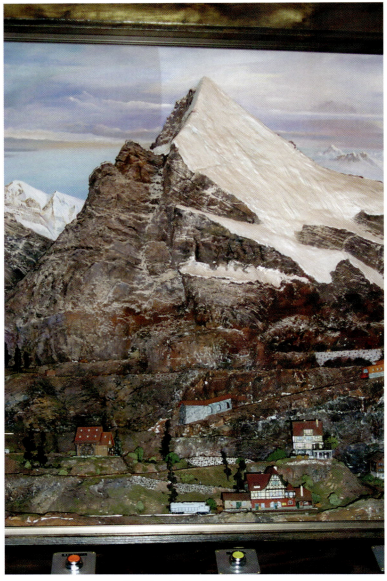

Part of train scene

The Old World Village 111

Castle in train diorama

As long as I'm in this area, I'll try one more shot to give a better idea of this panoramic view, although I can't show you what the buttons do. That would take a bit of magic that I don't have.

Bavarian village in train scene

Snoozing Geppetto

The Old World Village 113

From this point we proceed down to the street level. At the bottom of the steps is Geppetto sleeping. Watch closely and notice the old wood carver is breathing deeply as he sleeps. This scene depicts the story of how a wooden puppet becomes a real live boy. Occasionally the blue fairy makes an appearance to complete the scene. This room brings back memories of the story that many of us have read or heard of during our own childhood.

Blue fairy

Across the street is the Blackbird Bakery where the four and twenty blackbirds put on a performance for park guests. The large lead bird conducts the others as they sing and chatter with a cockney accent. Benches are available where visitors can sit and rest as they watch the show. There is a short wait between shows, but if the children can wait, they really like this event.

Blackbird Bakery

From here we will move on to an exclusive and artistically creative part of the village.

Chapter Eight
The Moods of Fantasy Fountains

Fantasy Fountains is a wonderful addition to the Enchanted Forest theme park. It is located in a building, the Jolly Roger, at one end of the Old World Village where visitors can get a snack, sit back, relax, and enjoy the program. This is a spectacular colored water show coordinated with mood setting music. The music and the colors blend together to lead the guests through many emotions. Often spectators are so spell bound that they applaud after the program to indicate their appreciation. The charm of this water spectacular is that it seems to be telling us a story with color and sound which has an appeal for all ages.

Upon entering the Jolly Roger where the Fantasy Fountains are located, guests may have to wait until the next show starts. Periodic announcements indicate how long the wait will be. But in the meantime why not grab a snack from the food service area. As show time approaches, the room lights start to dim. Colored lights begin to appear along the rock wall that forms a backdrop behind the fountains. The room becomes still as spectators focus on the scene developing in front of us. The spectacular story of lights, color, and dancing waters unfolds before our watchful eyes. However, the pictures shown here do not do justice to the beautiful feeling generated by the many moods of Fantasy Fountains as expressed in front of us. However, the photos will give the reader a brief idea of what can be seen.

The Jolly Roger

The Moods of Fantasy Fountains

Golden glory of water show

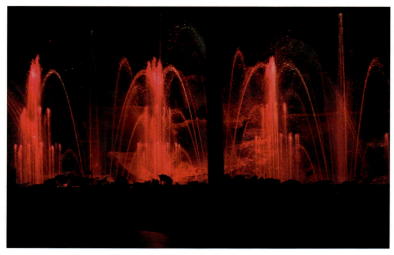

Dancing red fountains

Changing mood

Deep reverie

The Moods of Fantasy Fountains 119

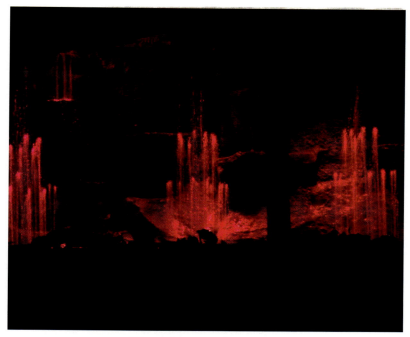

The dance changes

The waters sway rhythmically back and forth as the intensity of the dance increases. The audience is swept along as a metamorphosis takes place with the ever changing moods of the fountains. One has the feeling, for the moment, of being in another place and another time. There are times when the fountains appear to be like molten lava errupting from some underground cavern. Even the young children express their delight as the dance continues its flow. All eyes are on the show unfolding in front of them. Fantasy Fountains has become one of my favorite places in the park. Other visitors agree.

Grand display

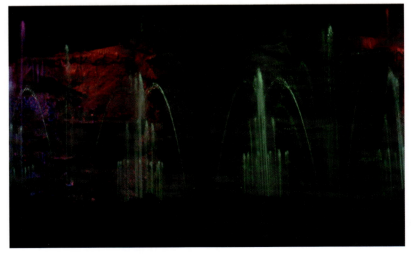

The mood darkens

The Moods of Fantasy Fountains 121

Somber purple

Wistful whites

122 Beyond the Castle

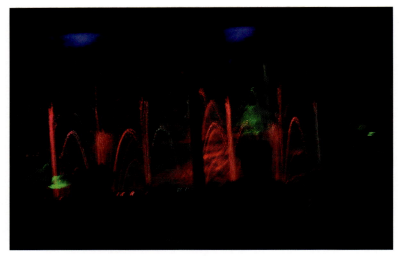

Changing flow

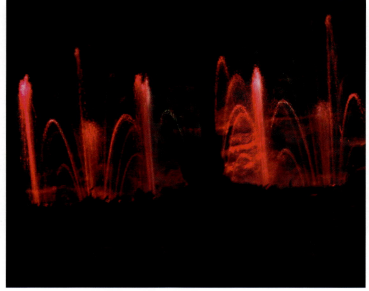

The show continues

The Moods of Fantasy Fountains 123

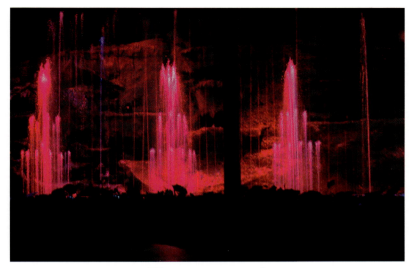

Finesse spread

Backdrop wall, mini fountains

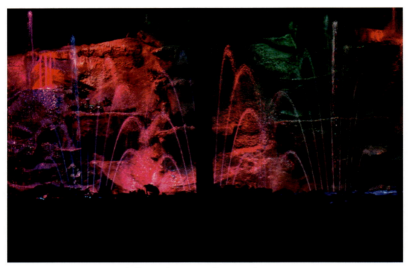

The dance broadens

Hovering waters

The Moods of Fantasy Fountains

Flowing movement tells the story

Changing lights

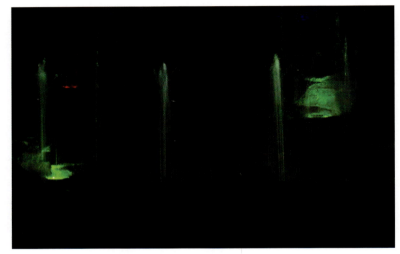

Wistful change

The dance brightens

These photos only give a suggestion of the beautiful evolving changes of the waters and can not capture the mood setting music. The quiet pastoral sounds change to a thunderous explosion of a rhythmic beat with a grand display telling its own story right before our eyes. It is something you have to see first hand to fully appreciate. From the somber to the serene, the moods are created for the visitors' pleasure. The shifting water patterns are an enjoyable sight. Such a delightful atmosphere is a great setting for a place to pause on your way through the park.

All men are creative but few are artists.

Paul Goodman (1911-1972)

Chapter Nine
Mother Nature

Picturesque forest view

Some of the greatest assets of the Enchanted Forest are its numerous natural treasures. There is the wealth of plant life and the abundance of small animals making their homes in the forest. On a hot summer day, visitors flock to the protective coolness of the park. In this setting, the trees offer shelter from the sweltering heat. Our guests can get relief, picnic, and have a family outing with things to do and places to explore. It's a great way to spend the dog days of summer.

There are several varieties of abundant plant life that can be found in our enchanted park. I will need the assistance of a more knowledgeable source to properly identify them. My scientific terminology would be limited to such clever descriptions as that squiggly purple flower, the plant with lacy leaves, the yucky brown stuff growing over there, and so forth.

Arched tree near upper log ride

Many hidden areas of the Enchanted Forest seem like the land that time forgot. These picturesque woods could have been the home of mythical beings such as elves, gnomes, unicorns, or any creature that the mind imagines. Possibly, a long time ago, this forest was even the home of ancient dinosaurs. Woodland spirits may still linger within the depths of our magical forest.

One can only stare at the surrounding vegetation and wonder. What if? Old bent branches or tree trunks dripping with hanging moss hint at what might have been or could be. It appears that a masterful artist was at work forming and shaping this natural wonderland.

Fascinating drooping branches

Deep in the forest, I spotted an unusual formation of thick, drooping branches. They were actually from some well hidden birch trees among the pines. Each seemed to be crowding the other for space and attention. It appears that there is always something new to enjoy with each visit to the Enchanted Forest.

Twisted stump near a construction area

Remains of aged tree

Wooded wonder

The wonders of nature are often taken for granted though it is always around us to enjoy. Hopefully, visitors will take a little time to appreciate the park's environment as well as its entertainment. The camera can not do justice to natures accomplishments. Mother Nature spreads her canvas, in all its glory, for its just rewards.

Bent Top near Ice Mountain

Natures painting

Let's keep walking. There are stranger creations to be found here. Look, what's that off to the left?

Robin's roost stump

There were some birds resting on this colorful stump but they flew away before I could take the picture. Well, that's the way the ball bounces. Shall we continue to see what else we might discover? It seems that I saw something earlier that was interesting and if I can find it again, I'll show it to you. We might even notice other interesting sights along the way. Other guests may see treasures that are not getting our attention. So, keep your eyes open. Where's the sight that caught my eye earlier! There it is, over there.

Stump garden

Mother Nature 139

Whimsical spider branches

These trees with spider branches are well hidden from most visitors. What fascinating designs their crooked branches form. What will be discovered next? In the realm of Mother Nature it is under her control. We are the seekers in her rich domain.

Dense beauty

Only a few splashes of sunlight find their mark on the ferns in this dense area. At one time a trail almost was established here but another spot proved more satisfactory. When the park's creative builder develops a section for visitors there are many decisions to be considered.

Sentinel stump

Sheltered ferns

Tunnel view

So far we have taken a look at trees, ferns, and notable stumps. However, nature shares other treasures with us such as flowers, animals, and birds. Many of these are located at the Enchanted Forest. The flowers change with the season and aren't always viewed by visitors.

At some time, a Johnny Appleseed of the plant world must have visited this woodland empire. Visitors can find such an abundant variety of plant life in this forest park. At different times, guests might see wild Columbine, Dogwood, the berries of Mountain Ash, wild

Strawberries, Daisies, Rhododendrons, and so forth. Colorful flowers add extra magic to the forest.

Berries of Mountain Ash

Mother Nature 145

Violet rules here

Petite white carpet

    This pristine forest is not open year around for a reason. Adverse weather conditions during the off season means some of the flowers will not be viewed by our visitors. The winter months can be cold, damp, and gloomy. Which means a visit at that time of the year would be rather miserable. Electrical wires, paint buckets, and work in progress would further deter winter visits. It is a period when workers prepare the park for the next season.

Flowers revealed by sunlight

148 Beyond the Castle

Rhododendron past its prime

Nature's mystical wonders are there to be enjoyed by all as visitors discover what the Enchanted Forest has to offer. There are places here that have been untouched by human hands for many years, adding to its hidden charm. While exploring the upper area of the log ride, I came upon a patch of tiny wild Daisies. They are very tiny and not seen by most of the park's guests.

Wild Daisies hidden near upper log ride flume

The forest around the upper section of Big Timber is not viewed by many. Therefore photos filmed in that part of the woods are rare. I only got up there because of my connections to the park. By exploring with a camera, I've investigated parts of our park that are also new to me.

In addition to vegetation, the Enchanted Forest is home to small woodland critters and a variety of birds that add to the crowning glory of nature. Chipmunks scamper swiftly, darting to snatch a crumb casually dropped from someone's lunch. The park squirrels seem to have had a group meeting and descend upon the picnic area en masse when dinner time approaches. They eagerly scurry around the tables looking for a handout, especially in the late afternoon when the pickings are good. These lively animals and their antics will be the subject for a future series of children's books about animals at the Enchanted Forest.

On this day, I am squirrel hunting with my ever ready camera. However, they act like they are aware of my intentions and quickly disappear as I approach. The ones that I spot seem to swiftly dart under the nearest bush. My mood is to think to myself; come out, come out wherever you are, you will-o-the-wisp rascals. There's movement in the bushes over there. Woops! A very little chipmunk just scooted across the trail. Phooey, he was too quick for me and my camera. I think my hunting is not so good today. Oh, well, another day and another time.

In addition to these ground critters, our fine feathered friends should be mentioned; otherwise known as "the birds". None are the product of an Alfred Hitchcock mystery. That reminds me of a day while roaming the trails that the Stellar Blue Jays were out in force and ruling the roost. They are very aggressive toward the other birds and chase them away. I didn't notice any of the other birds trying to stand up to the Jays. Their one redeeming factor is their beautiful color. There are a few of them out today and I have my camera ready.

Mother Nature 151

Colorful Blue Jay turns his back

Next, I decide to hike up to the theater because it's between shows and no one else is around. With the place to myself, I sit in the back row and wait quietly to see if anything stirs. Low and behold, soon I spot a small bird hopping out from the bushes, looking for food. My camera is poised and ready for action but my target disappears under one of the benches. In frozen awe, I watch for my chance. The little fellow is oblivious of my presence as he continues to move away. Finally, he reappears way down by the theater. I take aim. Gotcha!

Small Chickadee at theater

Mother Nature 153

Let me take you further down the trail because I thought there was movement high in the thick branches. There's a bird so well hidden that I almost missed him. With a little effort, I soon find him. His black feathers serve as camouflage, blending into the background. If he will only hold still long enough. Good. This feathered friend is so far away that he doesn't see me. Gotcha!

Blackbird hiding in protective branches

Beyond the Castle

Natures treasures are many and each visitor to the Enchanted Forest will be drawn to that which appeals to them. With the changing seasons there seems to be no end to the wonders of nature. Let's investigate a newer section that is being developed. It's not far from here.

Chapter Ten
Rides for the Young and More

    Up to now we have visited the big rides for the older youth and even for adults. Realizing there is another need to be satisfied, the Enchanted Forest expanded again to meet the challenge and a new section opened up. Young children love this special area where there are rides that are built with them in mind. This area is still expanding at the writing of this book. Little ones who can't enjoy the larger rides flock to this spot to participate in a fun thing that is just their size, much like their older siblings do elsewhere. This section is close to the theater and a crowd descends to these rides after the show is finished. An incidental feature is the nearby snack bar that is very handy on a hot day to solve the problem of the "thirsties".
    Even though this special area is still growing, children love what is there for them to enjoy. Sometimes it's a toss up whether the little ones want to see the theater first or go on the rides. The final decision is usually made by mom or dad. When they enter the children's small ride area, the youngsters rush to their favorite choice. This is their spot, they don't have to wait until they grow up. It's here, it's now, and it's for them. In the future, there will be more to come. The dreams of creation never stop even as the next generation of the park family becomes involved in its growth.

Frog Hopper

On the Frog Hopper, parents can join their children as they gleefully climb on for a ride. There is room for up to seven people on this ride. It rises upward in its own fashion to the delight of all. This means it moves in a sort of a herky-jerky manner. Of course, doting grandparents stand with their cameras ready. While some are enjoying the Frog Hopper, others line up for the ever popular bumper boats. Each child steers their own craft while trying to gently bump another's boat. This is where the little ones are in their element because they don't have to stand and wait for older ones in their family for now it is their turn. There is only one rider to each boat. A park employee wears waders in the boat pond to help the young visitors.

Garrett Baker riding boat

Garrett Baker decides to try his skills by steering one of the boats. Soon Garrett's brother climbs into a boat to join his younger sibling on the water. The park attendant makes sure his young riders are secure. This is something both boys can do as they roam together around the Enchanted Forest.

Austin Baker getting started

Big brother joins in the fun as he gets settled for a boat ride. The attendant is there to be sure all goes well. It's not a bad job on a warm summer day. Soon these two boys work up an appetite. I think their mind is set on some ice cream and they quickly find their way to the park ice cream parlor. Other children will end up at the picnic tables.

Rides for the Young and More 159

Children's Ferris wheel

When the picture of the Ferris wheel was taken, the workers were just getting ready to open for the day. As stated earlier, this area will be expanding and developing with more exciting things to do. After youngsters leave this section of the park, they are ready for snacks. In addition to playing, eating is another favorite pastime. There are several places around the park to accommodate this need. Visitors can use the main food service area with picnicing facilities, the theater snack bar, Fantasy Fountains snack bar, and the ever attractive Ice Cream parlor, and so forth.

Visitors picnic on a sunny day

Visitors can bring their own lunches or use the food service facilities in the park. After all with walking, going to the theater, going down slides, seeing Ice Mountain, visiting the Haunted House, and so forth; guests work up quite an appetite. Eating food, having drinks, and having ice cream are all part of the total picture of a fun day. Some groups have their members wear the same colored shirts, so they can better keep track of their group. The main idea is that they enjoy their visit to the Enchanted Forest.

Visitors at Children's area

It's time for our journey around the park to come to an end. I'll leave you with a few words about children.

Children are our most valuable natural resource.

—**Herbert Hoover** (1874-1964)

Chapter Eleven
Looking Back

    This business started on a shoe string through the desire of one man, Roger Tofte, to fulfill his dream. Still, the question is asked -why? It is not only the story of a dream, but it is also the story of free enterprise at work. Free enterprise was ingrained in our culture from the time we were little. Some children opened lemonade stands; others mowed lawns, babysat, or did various odd jobs. I especially remember another example. It was our own daughter, Susan, who was about five years old at the time. She put a crude paper sign in the front window saying, "restaurant open". It was not written that clearly, but I knew what she meant. Out of curiosity, I asked what she planned to serve her customers if any stopped by. Her eyes sparkled in childish delight, "water and ice cubes", was her eager reply. I carefully explained the pitfalls of her new business. Undaunted, our youngster moved on to other enterprises. Still, the desire was there. Our dreams and interests start from somewhere in our past. Past experiences are the building stones of our future. In this way, childhood memories help mold the character of the adult.
    Such was the case with my husband, Roger Tofte, as he grew up and developed his artistic skills and interests. He always had the desire to do something special with his many versatile talents.

When our family was young, we would pack up the children, hop into our bucket of bolts transportation, and drive to Minnesota to visit Roger's relatives. We tired during the long drive as the children grew restless. To our relief, there were roadside parks along the way where we could get out, stretch our legs, and have some fun at the same time. Roger thought about this and the seeds were planted. At that time, Oregon didn't have anything like this and the idea stirred Roger's imagination into overdrive. Why not? Maybe he would! Roger felt that he could develop a trail as good as the ones we had visited. After all, some of the ones we visited were very crude and he felt that he could be more creative if he put his mind to it. Our budding entrepreneur could be very meticulous when he strived for artistic quality. As a hungry man seeks food, so the creator of the Enchanted Forest sought his destiny. How was he to achieve these lofty goals? It wasn't going to be easy on our meager income and with a growing family.

Roger's idea couldn't begin to take shape until he was able obtain some land. On our meager income, it would take a while to get his project off the ground. The search for property began, just looking didn't cost anything. At the time, Roger worked as a draftsman for the state highway department. In his spare time, he repaired watches and did free lance art work. I also worked as a caseworker for the Marion County welfare office. The salaries in those days were very low and it was hard to make ends meet. But Roger would use the income from his watch repairing and art to put aside for his dream.

Finally in 1964, Roger purchased the land for fifty dollars a month until it was paid for a grand total of $4,000.00. To us it was a small fortune, but it was a start. The property was located in the wooded hills south of Salem, Oregon. Now the real work began as my husband grubbed around to clear enough space to work on his dream. The first structure to be built high up on the hill side was the Pumpkin for Peter, Pumpkin eater.

Peter and his Pumpkin, the first structure

This was how our real life fairy tale began. Once upon a time in the land of hopes and dreams, there was a young man seeking his future. In a land not so far away, he struggled against all odds. Through adverse weather conditions, few tools, purchases limited to funds on hand, Roger Tofte pushed on toward his dream. The struggle, at times, was overwhelming and his dream seemed to fade only to come back later, stronger than ever.

Undaunted, Roger worked for what seemed like an eternity. It took seven years of ups and downs while learning how to reach his goals. His persistence and drive even added to the mystique of the project. Young people and others were curious about the unusual activity in the woods. This generated stories about what was going on in the hillside south of Salem. Of course, none of them were true. One tale had him crashing a plane and landing in the forest where he started to build strange structures that to them had no rhyme or reason. These tales added spice to our life and gave us something to laugh about.

The Castle would be the entry point to the lower trail and at first there was nothing to see from the road. When he started work on the front where the castle would be, even newspaper reporters were getting curious about this unusual project in the hills. It would stand for his dream world and would be noticed by those driving by. People often thought it was the first structure to be built because it was the first to be seen. While Roger's dream was being built, it represented his castle in the clouds.

Castle in the clouds, one man's dream

    Roger's fairy tale venture was well under way, but progress would be slow, mostly due to lack of funds. He would repair a few watches, then buy a bag of cement, and so forth. It was a tremendous challenge. Our youngest child was born two years into his project and with four little ones to care for; I had to quite my job for the welfare office. After years of struggle, when the children were ages five, nine, twelve, and fifteen; we all pitched in to get the entrance building ready to open. It took two days, but we were finally ready to open the trail through the woods on August 8, 1971. It should be noted that since then, the Enchanted Forest hasn't stopped growing to this day. A more detailed history of the family and the beginning years of our trials and triumphs can be read in the book, *The Enchanted Forest and Its Family.*

    When we first opened "Mary Had a Little Lamb" was one of the original structures on the lower trail. Roger built the small house at our home along with other smaller items, such as cement mushrooms and other fairyland figures. However, moving these items to the Enchanted Forest was a real challenge. Roger decided to build the rest of the scenes at the property, not our home. Our children thought everybody's dad did things like that. When we first opened, the original work crew consisted of our family and two friends of our daughter. Each had their work duties, including our five year old. But most of her time was spent playing near me in the entrance building.

Mary had a little lamb

For every artist or craftsman each new undertaking is a challenge. Although this wooded wonderland started as a trail through the woods, the status quo was always changing. It was a matter of completing one project and then move on to the next level. There's an old saying, "a rolling stone gathers no moss". There was no time to become stagnant at the Enchanted Forest, the park was always changing. Roger created this family theme park, but as time passed and the park grew, so did our family. Their involvement increased as they contributed their talents to the development of this unique theme park south of Salem, Oregon. The talents and skills of our children added to the possibilities of what could be accomplished.

Another building of interest is the original hot dog stand. The lunch hut we purchased was a small eight by eight foot stand with no glass windows and just an opening where the door was. It was painted brilliant orange. Our nine year old daughter, Mary, was the first one to run the hot dog stand but the cold wind blew through the window and door openings. As soon as we had enough money, glass windows were added and a real door put in. Our fare was simple; hot dogs, chips, pop, and coffee. As sections were added to the building, the variety of items served increased.

Original lunch hut, after expansion

Each new undertaking was a challenge. After the lower trail, the shoe slide, and the western town; the first major project to have an additional charge was the Haunted House. Up to this point, we had never tried such a large building project within the park. Our son had an interest in electronics and robotics and this undertaking gave him a chance to add his skills to that of his dad. Roger's talents did not include this field in his repertoire. The house loomed above the walls surrounding the Tofteville western town. Its livery stable doors were closed and work on the newest structure continued on the other side out of sight for most visitors.

But all the bustle and activity on the other side of the high walls aroused our guests' curiosity. We were bombarded with their questions. What's going on? What is it? When will it open? They did manage to see the upper part of the building above the Tofteville fence. This only piqued visitors' interest and increased the questions. When opening day finally arrived, crowds gathered at the livery stable doors and once the massive gates swung open, they would never close again. The excitement was contagious and we were swept along in the electricity of the moment. We could hardly wait to see the reaction when the first visitors would enter the Enchanted Forest Haunted House. We also had questions. What would they think? Did they enjoy it? What would our guests say? None of us were disappointed, owners and visitors. The heartfelt response was our reward.

Walk to Haunted house

Haunted House, a different look

Other major construction projects were Ice Mountain, the Old World Village, Big Timber, the young children's ride area, and so forth. Not to be overlooked is the Fairweather Theater which is free to our guests. Through it all, we are still learning as we grow.

Castle mural 2001

Chapter Twelve
New Visions

    Where would we be without our old dreams and new visions? The Enchanted Forest exists because of one man's dreams and continues to grow with input from the next generation. The growth of the Tofte family adds dimension to the park's future. The visionary developments now include such fields as theater, music, robotics, business promotion, better office procedures, safety, maintenance, and new construction. We have entered the age of digital devices and computers. The new world is changing as is the Enchanted Forest. However, park growth means an increase in park maintenance, more personnel, and increased responsibilities in park operations. The simple has become complex but it's an amazing world that we live in.

    After the Enchanted Forest closes for the season, activity in the park shifts into another gear. It is a time of attending to the nitty gritty work of business operations, such as future advertising, taxes, personnel, inventory, ordering merchandise and supplies and so forth. The pros and cons have to be weighed on the management of finances and what can be allotted for new construction and needed refurbishing. As you can see the office personnel and administration have their work cut out and it has to be accomplished within the allotted time as the park prepares to open for the next season. The maintenance and construction workers also have to meet the new season deadline. Usually there is a tendency to relax after closing with the feeling that there is plenty of time. However, the clock ticks swiftly and after the holidays, everyone moves into a more frantic, hectic pace as they try to get ready for the March fifteenth opening date. Life in the office becomes a beehive of activity.

Susan Vaslev

Mary Tofte

Throughout the park there are sounds of work in progress. If weather permits, the noise of motors, hammers, and saws echo through the forest. More subdued is the gentle swish of the paint brushes bringing life back to faded structures. Those conducting business at the Enchanted Forest may even hear the groaning sounds of a cement mixer straining to keep up with the demands for its service. Of course new construction is what makes new visions become a reality. There are works in progress and works on the drawing board. It seems that the park is constantly in transition.

Ken Tofte in shop

Some of the park changes are for the convenience of our guests. One sample of this effort to improve facilities was the recent addition of a stroller path to the theater. The steps to the theater were difficult to maneuver for those who had little ones in strollers. It was exhausting to carry those bulky strollers up the steps so the family could watch the show. Therefore, our workers cleared a slopping path bypassing the theater steps and finished it with paver stones. It was an improvement that met with approval by our park guests.

Stroller path under construction

The added facility is appreciated by more than families with small children. It's also useful for the handicapped who can't maneuver the steps. I came back later and was able to see the finished path which is shown in the following picture.

Completed path

Near the children's ride area, there is a new section under construction at the time this book is being written. Bustling activity indicates the push to get this new project ready for the 2002 season. The cushioned bumper car ride is attracting attention even before it is ready for customers. I rode one of the test cars at a dealer's display area and really enjoyed it in spite of my arthritic knees. A ride like this can be a lot of old fashioned fun!

Clearing for new construction

A different view

With my camera I will try to capture different stages of development for the new attraction. Our workers anticipate the end result as much as we do. There is always speculation about who will be testing our new rides before they are approved for our customers. As we all discover, from the bare ground up, it is interesting to watch each project as it takes shape.

Workers at new site

Fortunately, we were able to purchase used cars for the ride. We have skilled personnel who are able to renovate them for our use. These are stacked to one side of the clearing, out of the way, while a new surface is prepared for their use. A building will be erected where cars can be prepared for refurbishing. One has to use their imagination to envision the finished product. Our crew is working tooth and nail to get this ride ready for our visitors. Some who have already heard about it can hardly wait to initiate it.

Construction in progress

With adverse weather coming in, plastic was laid over the future floor to protect it. Once the floor has set up we don't have to worry about such things. There may even be a shelter provided over the area for protection of riders and cars from Oregon rain. The smooth floor will make movement easier as drivers bump and bang with each other. Construction takes patience and input from our capable workers. These bumper cars can hit and spin as they recoil from others on the floor. A little daring and concentration will make this ride a fun thing to do. In the meantime, another season approaches. Will this ride be ready on time for the start of the season or will it open later into the summer? Everyone is doing their best, but you never know until it is actually done.

Construction in progress, 2001

Lumber ready for use

Forms near mixer

Ride floor goes around this tree

186 Beyond the Castle

An interesting feature is a tree growing at one end of the floor. The bumper cars can whip around this ingrown obstacle. It should make the ride very interesting and add to the visitors' enjoyment.

Cars waiting to be renovated

The men are hard at work renovating the cars and have taken off the rubber tubes to do their work. At this time two of our workers have this responsibility. As soon as the first car is ready, I know a few people who want to try it out. But renovating takes time and our visitors will have to wait until it is completed. Then they can have their turn.

New Visions 187

Working on the cars

Testing the car without tubing

After a few test drives, there is more fine tuning and adjusting to improve the cars drive unit. I'm sure there will be more testing before all units are ready for our park visitors.

Adjusting the new car

Roger Tofte supervising

Other ideas are being developed for the future. By now our guests realize the Enchanted Forest is a work in progress. As far as the future goes, there are plans for a ride through the land of gnomes and elves. The park also needs a new larger gift shop to ease the congestion in our current accommodations. Shopping is one of the pleasures most visitors enjoy in visiting a theme park like the Enchanted Forest. Whatever is in the future you can be sure the Tofte family will be involved.

Do what you can, with what you have, where you are.
— **Theodore Roosevelt** (1858-1919)

ABOUT THE AUTHOR

　　　Mavis Tofte always dreamed of being a writer. But the facts of life postponed the inevitable. She had a few obligations to tend to first. Mavis was a member of the National Honor Society and received the Scholastic gold key art award while in high school. This was followed by earning an AB degree from Willamette University in 1953, majoring in Sociology. After graduating, she worked as a caseworker for the Marion County Welfare office which was located in Salem, Oregon. Mavis was married in 1954 and they had four children. If this wasn't enough, while her husband was fulfilling his dream of creating the Enchanted Forest, she not only worked there but also managed the business. The demands of these activities left little time for other interests. However, it gave her a great wealth of material and knowledge of people for her to use later when the time was right for Mavis to follow her desire to become a writer. A wonderful new world lay at her fingertips.

Book order form

Creative Quill
460 Myers S
Salem, Or. 97302
Ph #503-363-2843

Books available:
Select Books desired

☐ *The Enchanted Forest and Its Family,*
   ISBN 0-9709906-0-X
   $16.95 per book plus S&H $2.00

☐ *Beyond the Castle, the Enchanted Forest,*
   ISBN 0-9709906-2-8
   $19.95 per book plus S&H $2.00

*Please remit total amount due with order,
payable to* **Creative Quill.**

Mailing address:

Name _____

Street _____

City _____ State _____ Zip _____

Name of book _____

_____

Number of books _____ @ $16.95 = Total _____

Number of books _____ @ $19.95 = Total _____

Plus shipping & handling _____

Total Amount Due = $ _____